# PICKLE
# PRICK

↑↑↑↑↑↑
↑↑↑↑↑↑
↑↑↑↑↑↑
↑↑↑↑↑↑

# This
# Bitch

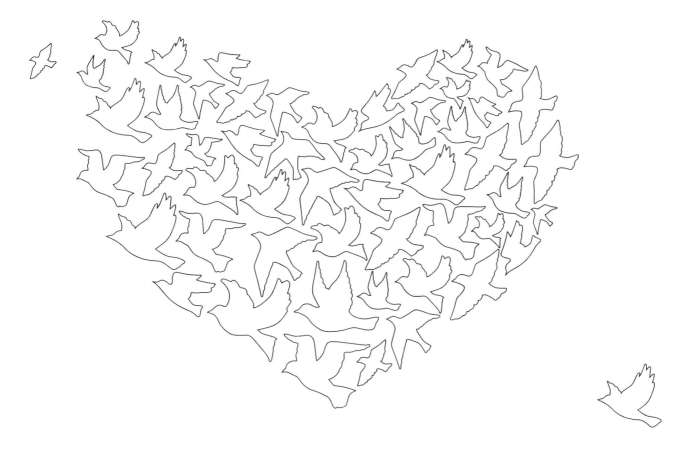

STOP FOR A MOMENT,
CLOSE YOUR EYES,
AND BREATHE.

FART GARGLER

# CUM
# WALLOWER

# CAPTAIN
# DICK WAD

# CARPE SCROTUM

# BABA GA DOUCHE

54167504R00025

Made in the USA
Charleston, SC
29 March 2016